British Citizenship Test
Study Guide

The essential study guide for the Life in the UK Test

....

Published by Red Squirrel Publishing

Red Squirrel Publishing

Suite 235, 77 Beak Street,

London, W1F 9DB, United Kingdom

sales@redsquirrelbooks.com

www.redsquirrelbooks.com

Third Impression

ISBN 0 9552159 19

ISBN 978 0 9552159 19

Designed and artworked by
Cox Design Partnership, Witney, Oxon

Printed and bound in Europe by
the Alden Group, Oxford

CONTENTS

INTRODUCTION

This publication is a study guide for candidates intending to take the *Life in the UK Test*. Before you start, take time to read through this section so that you get the most out of this guide.

The background material in this guide has been reproduced from the *'Life in the United Kingdom: A Journey to Citizenship'* handbook published by the Home Office. The *Life in the UK Test* focuses on content from chapters 2, 3, and 4 of this publication – only these chapters have been reproduced in this guide.

The sample questions included in this guide are intended as a supplementary aid to help you prepare for the *Life in the UK* test. They are not exactly the same questions that you will be asked during your test, although they cover the same content. They are intended to help give you confidence and provide you with feedback while you prepare for your test.

Check our website (www.redsquirrelbooks.com) for the latest updates to this book and for extra study tips. If you have any thoughts on how we can improve this publication then we'd be very keen to hear from you. You can email your thoughts to us at feedback@redsquirrelbooks.com

Good luck with your test.

A CHANGING SOCIETY

Migration to Britain

If we go back far enough in time, almost everyone living in Britain today may be seen to have their origins elsewhere. We are a nation of immigrants – able to trace our roots to countries throughout Europe, Russia, the Middle East, Africa, Asia and the Caribbean. In the past immigrant groups came to invade and to seize land. More recently, people have come to Britain to find safety and in search of jobs and a better life.

Britain is proud of its tradition of providing a safe haven for people fleeing persecution and conflict. In the sixteenth and seventeenth centuries, Protestant Huguenots from France came to Britain to escape religious persecution. The terrible famine in Ireland in the mid 1840s led to a surge of migration to the British mainland, where Irish labourers provided much of the workforce for the construction of canals and railways.

Between 1880–1910, large numbers of Jewish people came to Britain from what are now Poland, Ukraine, and Belarus to escape the violence they faced at home. Unhappily, in the 1930s, fewer were able to leave Germany and central Europe in time to escape the Nazi Holocaust, which claimed the lives of 6 million people.

Migration since 1945

At the end of the Second World War, there was the huge task of rebuilding Britain after six years of war. With not enough people available for work, the British government encouraged workers from other parts of Europe to help with the process of reconstruction. In 1948, the invitation was extended to people in Ireland and the West Indies.

A shortage of labour in Britain continued throughout the 1950s and some UK industries launched advertising campaigns to attract workers from overseas. Centres were set up in the West Indies to recruit bus crews, and textile and engineering firms in the north of England and the Midlands sent agents to find workers in India and Pakistan. For about 25 years people from the West Indies, India, Pakistan and later Bangladesh, travelled to work and settle in Britain.

In the 1970s migration from these areas fell after the Government passed new laws restricting immigration to Britain. However, during this period, Britain admitted 28,000 people of Indian origin who had been forced to leave Uganda, and 22,000 refugees from South East Asia. In the 1980s, the largest immigrant groups were from the United States, Australia, South Africa, New Zealand, Hong Kong, Singapore and Malaysia.

With the fall of the Iron Curtain and the break-up of the Soviet Union in the late 1980s and early 90s, other groups began to come to Britain, seeking a new and safer way of life. Since 1994 there has been a rise in the numbers moving to Britain from Europe, the Middle East, Asia, Africa and the Indian sub-continent, many of whom have sought political asylum. Migrants to Britain, however, face increasingly tighter controls, as the Government attempts to prevent unauthorised immigration and to examine more closely the claims of those seeking asylum.

The changing role of women

In nineteenth century Britain, families were usually large and, in most households, men, women, and children all contributed towards the family wage. Although they were economically very important, women in Britain had fewer rights in law than men. Until 1857, a married woman had no right to divorce her husband, and until 1882 a woman's earnings, along with any property or money she brought to the marriage, automatically belonged to her husband.

In the late nineteenth and early twentieth centuries, an increasing number of women campaigned and demonstrated for greater rights and, in particular, the right to vote. However, the protests and demonstrations were halted during the First World War, as women joined in the war effort and took on a much greater variety of work than they had done before. Women (over the age of 30) were finally given the right to vote and to stand for election for Parliament after the War had ended in 1918. It wasn't until 1928 that women in Britain received voting rights at the same age as men.

Despite these improvements, women still faced discrimination in the workplace. When a woman married, it was quite common for her to be asked to leave work by her employer. Many jobs were closed to women, and women found it very difficult to enter university. The 1960s and 70s saw increasing pressure from women for equal rights and, during this period, laws were passed giving women the right to equal pay and prohibiting employers from discriminating against women because of their sex.

Women in Britain today

Women in Britain make up 51 per cent of the population, and 45 per cent of the workforce. Girls, as a whole, leave school today with better qualifications than boys, and there are now more women than men at university. Employment opportunities for women now are much greater than they were in the past. Although women continue to be employed in traditionally female areas, such as health care, teaching, secretarial, and sales, there is strong evidence that attitudes are changing and that women are doing a much wider range of work than before.

Research shows that today very few people believe that women in Britain should stay at home and not go out to work. Today, almost three-quarters of women with children of school age are in paid work.

In many households, women continue to have a major share in childcare and housework, but here too there is evidence of greater equality, with fathers taking an increasing role in raising the family and household chores. Despite this progress, many argue that more needs to be done to achieve greater equality between women and men – particularly in the workplace. Women in Britain do not have the same access as men to promotion and better-paid jobs, and the average hourly rate of pay for women is about 20 per cent lower than it is for men.

Children, family and young people

In Britain there are almost 15 million children and young people up to the age of 19. This represents almost a quarter of the UK population. Young people are considered to be a group with their own identity, interests, and fashions that in some ways distinguish them from older people. Generally speaking, once they reach adulthood, children tend to move away from the family home, but this varies from one family and one community to another. Most children in Britain receive weekly pocket money from their parents, and many get more for doing jobs around the house.

Children today in the UK do not play outside the home as much as they did in the past. Home entertainment, such as television, videos and computers, are seen as part of the reason for this, but so also is an increased concern for children's safety. Incidents of child molestation by strangers are often reported in great detail, but there is no evidence that dangers of this kind are increasing.

As a result of changing attitudes towards divorce and separation, family patterns in Britain have also changed considerably in the last 20 years. Today while 65 per cent of children live with both birth parents, almost 25 per cent live in lone parent families, and 10 per cent live within a stepfamily.

Education

The Government places great importance on the need to assess and test pupils in order to know what they have achieved. Compulsory testing takes place at the ages of seven, eleven and fourteen in England and Scotland (but not in Wales where more informal methods are assessment are favoured). These tests help to give parents a good indication of their children's progress and children know the subjects they are doing well and those that need extra attention.

Most young people take GCSE (General Certificate of Secondary Education) examinations at sixteen, and many take vocational qualifications, A/S and A levels (Advanced levels), at seventeen and eighteen.

One in three young people now move onto higher education after school. The Government aim is to reach one in two. Of those that do, some defer their university entrance by taking a year out. This often includes periods doing voluntary work, travelling overseas, or earning money to pay for fees and living expenses at university.

Work

It is now common for young people to have a part-time job whilst they are still at school. Recent estimates suggest that there are two million children at work at any one time. The most common jobs are newspaper delivery and work in supermarkets and newsagents. Many parents believe that part-time work of this kind helps children to become more independent, as well as providing them (and sometimes their family) with extra income.

It is important to note, however, that the employment of children is strictly controlled by law, and that there are concerns for the safety of children who work illegally or are not properly supervised.

Health hazards

Many parents in Britain worry that their children may misuse addictive substances and drugs in some way.

Cigarette consumption in Britain has fallen significantly and now only a minority of the population smoke. Restrictions are planned against smoking in public places. Smoking has declined amongst young people as well as adults, although statistics show that girls smoke more than boys. Tobacco, by law, should not be sold to anyone under the age of 16.

Alcohol abuse is a problem. Although young people below the age of 18 are not allowed by law to buy alcohol, there is concern in Britain over the age at which some young people start drinking, and the amount of alcohol that they consume in one session or 'binge'. Increasing penalties including on-the-spot fines are being introduced to help control this.

Controlled drugs are illegal drugs. It is an offence in Britain to possess, produce, or supply substances such as heroin, cocaine, ecstasy, amphetamines, and cannabis. However, current statistics indicate that half of young adults, and about a third of the population as a whole, have used illegal drugs at one time or another – if sometimes only as an experiment.

There is a well-established link between the use of hard drugs (eg crack cocaine and heroin) and crime, and it is widely accepted that drug misuse carries a huge social and financial cost to the country. Much crime, such as burglary or stealing in the street by threat or violence (called mugging) is associated with wanting money for drugs. The task of finding an effective way of dealing with this problem is an important issue facing British society.

Young people's attitudes and action

Young people in Britain are able to vote in elections from the age of 18. However, in the 2001 general election, only one in five potential first-time voters actually cast their vote, and there has been a great debate over the reasons for this. Researchers have concluded that one reason is young people's distrust of politicians and the political process.

Although many young people show little interest in party politics, there is strong evidence that they are interested in some specific political issues. Those who commonly say they are not interested in politics at all often express strong concern about environmental issues and cruelty to animals.

A survey of the attitudes of young people in England and Wales in 2003 revealed that crime, drugs, war/terrorism, racism, and health were the five most important issues that they felt Britain faced today. The same survey asked young people about their participation in political and community events. It was reported that 86 per cent of young people had taken part in some form of community activity over the past year. 50 per cent had taken part in fund-raising or collecting money for charity.

REVISION QUESTIONS

Test your understanding of this section by completing the questions below.
Check your answers on page 55

1	List some of the reasons why migrants have come to the UK ANSWER:
2	What sort of work have migrants done? ANSWER:
3	What were immigrants from Ireland and the West Indies invited into the UK to do? ANSWER:
4	Name three countries that Jewish people migrated to the UK from, to escape persecution during 1880–1910 ANSWER:
5	Which countries were invited to provide immigrant workers to help British reconstruction after World War II? ANSWER:
6	What year did women gain the right to divorce their husband in the UK? ANSWER:
7	When did women first get the right to vote? ANSWER:
8	Are there more men or women in study at university? ANSWER:
9	What percentage of the workforce are women? ANSWER:
10	What proportion of women with children (of school age) also work? ANSWER:
11	What is the percentage difference in pay between male and female hourly pay rates? ANSWER:

12	How many young people (up to the age of 19) are there in the UK?
	ANSWER:

13	What percentage of children live in single parent families or step families?
	ANSWER:

14	When do children take tests at school?
	ANSWER:

15	How many young people enrol to go on to higher education?
	ANSWER:

16	How many children (under 18) are estimated to be working in the United Kingdom at any time?
	ANSWER:

17	What are the minimum ages for buying alcohol and tobacco?
	ANSWER:

18	In the 2001 general election, what proportion of first time voters actually cast their vote?
	ANSWER:

BRITAIN TODAY: A PROFILE

Population

In 2001, the population of the United Kingdom was recorded at just under 59 million people.

Table 1: United Kingdom Population 2001

England	49.1 million	83%	UK population
Scotland	5.1 million	9%	UK population
Wales	2.9 million	5%	UK population
Northern Ireland	1.7 million	3%	UK population
Total : United Kingdom	**58.8 million**		

Source: National Statistics

More information on the 2001 Census is available from the Government Statistics website, www.statistics.gov.uk

Since 1951, the population has grown by 17 per cent. This is lower than the average growth for countries in the European Union (which is 23 percent), and much smaller than some other countries, such as the USA (80 per cent), and Australia (133 per cent).

The UK birth rate was at an all time low in 2002 and, although it rose slightly in 2003, Britain now has an ageing population. For the first time, people aged 60 and over form a larger part of the population than children under 16. There is also a record number of people aged 85 and over.

Although there has been a general increase in population in the UK over the last 20 years, the growth has not been uniform, and some areas, such as the North East and North West of England have experienced a decline.

The Census

A census of the population in Britain has been taken every ten years since 1801 (with the exception of 1941, when Britain was at war). The next census will be in 2011.

When a census takes place, a census form is delivered to households throughout the country, and by law must be completed. The form asks for a lot of information to ensure that official statistics about the population are accurate, but is all completely confidential and anonymous as regards each individual. Only after 100 years can the records be consulted freely.

Ethnic diversity

The largest ethnic minority in Britain are people of Indian descent. These are followed by those of Pakistani descent, of mixed ethnic descent, Black Caribbean descent, Black African descent, and Bangladeshi descent. Together these groups make up 7.9 per cent of the UK population.

Today, about half the members of the African Caribbean, Pakistani, Indian, and Bangladeshi communities were born in Britain. Considerable numbers of people of Chinese, Italian, Greek and Turkish Cypriot, Polish, Australian, Canadian, New Zealand and American descent are also resident within the UK.

Table 2 : United Kingdom Population Ethnic Groups 2001

Total Population			
White	54.2 million	92.0%	UK population
Mixed	0.7 million	1.2%	UK population
Asian or Asian British			
Indian	1.1 million	1.8%	UK population
Pakistani	0.7 million	1.3%	UK population
Bangladeshi	0.3 million	0.5%	UK population
Other Asian	0.2 million	0.4%	UK population
Black or Black British			
Black Caribbean	0.6 million	1.0%	UK population
Black African	0.5 million	0.8%	UK population
Black Other	0.1 million	0.2%	UK population
Chinese	0.2 million	0.4%	UK population
Other	0.2 million	0.4%	UK population

Source: National Statistics from the 2001 census

Where do people live?

Most members of ethnic minority groups live in England, where they make up nine per cent of the total population. This compares with two per cent each in Wales and Scotland, and less than one per cent in Northern Ireland.

45 per cent of the population of ethnic minorities live in the London area, where they comprise 29 per cent of all residents. Most other member of ethnic minorities in Britain live in one of four other areas: the West Midlands, the South East, the North West, and Yorkshire and Humberside.

REVISION QUESTIONS

Test your understanding of this section by completing the questions below.
Check your answers on page 55

19	What was the population of the United Kingdom in 2001?
	ANSWER:

20	How much has the UK population grown by (in percentage terms) since 1951?
	ANSWER:

21	What is the population of Northern Ireland?
	ANSWER:

22	What is the population of Wales?
	ANSWER:

23	What is the population of Scotland?
	ANSWER:

24	When was the first census carried out in the United Kingdom?
	ANSWER:

25	When will the next UK census be carried out?
	ANSWER:

26	Why was a census not carried out in the United Kingdom in 1941?
	ANSWER:

27	How often is a census carried out in the United Kingdom?
	ANSWER:

28	How many years must have passed before an individual's census form is viewable by the public?
	ANSWER:

29	What percentage of the United Kingdom's population is made up of ethnic minorities?
	ANSWER:
30	What is the largest ethnic minority in Britain?
	ANSWER:
31	What overall proportion of today's African Caribbean, Pakistani, Indian, and Bangladeshi communities in Britain were born there?
	ANSWER: about half
32	What percentage of London's residents are ethnic minorities?
	ANSWER:
33	What percentage of UK's ethnic minorities live in the London area?
	ANSWER:

Religion and tolerance

Everyone in Britain has the right to religious freedom. Although Britain is historically a Christian society, people are usually very tolerant towards the faiths of others and those who have no religious beliefs.

In the 2001 Census, just over 75 per cent of the UK population reported that they had a religion. More than seven people out of ten stated that this was Christian. Nearly three per cent of the population described their religion as Muslim, and one per cent as Hindu. After these, the next largest religious groups are Sikhs, Jews, and Buddhists.

Although many people in Britain have a religious belief, this is not always matched by regular attendance at services. It is estimated that regular church attendance in England is between eight and eleven per cent of the population. Church attendance in Scotland however, although declining, is almost twice the level for England and Wales.

The established church

The Church of England, or Anglican Church as it is also known, came into existence in 1534. The King installed himself as head of the Church, and the title of Supreme Governor has been held by the King or Queen ever since.

The monarch at the coronation is required to swear to maintain the Protestant Religion in the United Kingdom, and heirs to the throne are not allowed to marry anyone who is not Protestant. The Queen or King also has the right to appoint a number of senior church officers, including the Archbishop of Canterbury, who is the head of the Church. In practice however, the Prime Minister makes this selection on the recommendation of a special committee appointed by the Church.

Other Christian groups

Further splits in the Church took place after the Reformation, giving rise to a number of different Protestant denominations. These included the Baptists, Presbyterians, and the Society of Friends (or Quakers), all of which continue today. In the eighteenth century the Methodist movement developed, working in particular amongst poorer members of society.

In Wales today, Baptists and Methodists are the two most widespread denominations. In Scotland there are more than a million members of the Presbyterian Church, the established Church of Scotland, known as the Kirk.

About ten per cent of the population of Britain are Roman Catholic.

The regions of Britain

Britain is a relatively small country. The distance from the north coast of Scotland to the south cost of England is approximately 600 miles (almost 1,000 km), and it is about 320 miles (just over 500 km) across the widest part of England and Wales. However, nowhere in Britain is more than 75 miles (120 km) from the coast.

Many people remark on the great variety in the British landscape. In the space of a few hours it is possible to travel from a major cosmopolitan city to historic sites, old cathedrals, villages, moors and mountains.

Regional differences

In one respect, almost every part of Britain is the same. A common language, national newspapers, radio, and television, and shops with branches throughout the United Kingdom mean that everybody, to some degree, shares a similar culture. However beneath the increasingly standardised appearance of our city centres and suburbs, there are real diversities and cultural differences between different parts of the United Kingdom.

Possibly the two most distinctive areas of Britain are Wales and Scotland. Both have their own language. Welsh is taught in schools and widely spoken in north and west Wales. Gaelic is still spoken in the Highlands and Islands of Scotland. Many people believe that the Welsh and the Scots have a stronger sense of identity and culture than the English – perhaps brought about by their struggle to stay independent. The creation of the Assembly for Wales and the Scottish Parliament in 1999 has led some people to suggest that England needs its own parliament and there is now considerable discussion about what is a distinctive English identity.

Accents are a clear indication of regional differences in Britain. Geordie, Scouse, and Cockney are well known dialects from Tyneside, Liverpool, and London respectively, but other differences in speech exist in all parts of the country. Scottish and Welsh speech is distinctive, and varies within those two countries. In some areas a person's accent will indicate where they are from, within a distance of twenty miles.

Regional differences also exist in the styles of buildings and the materials used in their construction. Thatched cottages, much less common than they once were, are mainly products of the south, the south-west and east of England. Older buildings are usually made from local stone, giving houses in North Yorkshire, Derbyshire, and many other places a unique appearance.

The industrial legacy of regions also gives rise to distinct styles of architecture. The mill towns of northern England are good examples of this. The insularity of some communities, particularly on the coast and in remote corners of Britain, has meant that their appearance has changed very little in the past 50 years. In contrast, other areas, whose traditional industries have been replaced by others, are almost unrecognisable from what they were a generation ago.

REVISION QUESTIONS

Test your understanding of this section by completing the questions below.
Check your answers on page 56

34 According to the 2001 Census, what percentage of people stated their religion as Christian?

ANSWER:

35 According to the 2001 Census, what percentage of people stated their religion as Muslim?

ANSWER:

36 According to the 2001 Census, what percentage of the UK population reported that they had a religion?

ANSWER:

37 What year did the Church of England come in existence?

ANSWER:

38 Which other name can be used to refer to the Church of England?

ANSWER:

39 What is the title of the King or Queen within the Church of England

ANSWER:

40 Who is the head of the Church of England?

ANSWER:

41 Who appoints the Archbishop of Canterbury?

ANSWER:

42 What must a monarch swear to maintain as part of their coronation?

ANSWER:

43 According to the Church of England, heirs to the throne are not allowed to marry who?

ANSWER:

44 What is the Church of Scotland also known as?

ANSWER:

45	What percentage of the British population are Roman Catholic?
	ANSWER:

46	What is the distance of the widest part across England and Wales?
	ANSWER:

47	What is the distance from the north coast of Scotland to the south coast of England?
	ANSWER:

48	Where is the Welsh language spoken?
	ANSWER:

49	Where is the Gaelic language spoken?
	ANSWER:

50	In which year were the Assembly for Wales and the Scottish Parliament created?
	ANSWER:

51	What are the two most widespread Christian denominations in Wales?
	ANSWER:

52	Where are Cockney dialects spoken?
	ANSWER:

53	Where are Scouse dialects spoken?
	ANSWER:

54	Where are Geordie dialects spoken?
	ANSWER:

Customs and traditions

Tourist guides commonly paint a view of a rural Britain that is not always recognisable to those who live here. The countryside is regarded by many as 'real England', but in fact, the great majority of people live in cities or their suburbs. People's lives in the UK, like many others throughout the world, are a mixture of the old and the new. City dwellers love to visit the countryside. But the abolition of fox hunting, regarded by many city dwellers as long overdue, has been bitterly contested by most country dwellers who see it as a denial of their values and traditions.

Festivals and other traditions continue to exist in all parts of the country, but their existence depends almost entirely on the continued support of those who live in the local community.

Sport

Sport of all kind plays a major part in many people's lives. Football, rugby, and cricket all have a large following, and success on the sporting field is a great source of local and national pride. Major sporting events, such as the Grand National horse race, the Football Association (FA) Cup Final, and the Wimbledon tennis championships, capture the attention of many people in Britain, including those who do not normally follow these sports.

National days

National days are not celebrated in Britain in the same way as they are in a number of other countries. Only in Northern Ireland (and the Republic of Ireland) is St Patrick's Day taken as an official holiday. The greatest celebrations are normally reserved for the New Year and the Christian festivals of Christmas and Easter.

National Days

1st March	St David's Day, the national day of Wales
17th March	St Patrick's Day, the national day of both Northern Ireland and the Republic of Ireland
23rd April	St George's Day, the national day of England
30th November	St Andrew's Day, the national day of Scotland

There are also four public holidays a year, called Bank Holidays, when legislation requires banks and most businesses to close. These are of no nationalistic or religious significance.

Religious and traditional festivals

Most religious festivals in Britain are based on the Christian tradition, but also widely recognised are customs and traditions such as Eid ul-Fitr, Divali and Yom Kippur, belonging to other religions. Many of these are explained to children in all the schools as part of their lessons in religious education; and they are celebrated by followers of these faiths in their communities.

The main Christian and traditional festivals

Christmas Day, December 25th, celebrates the birth of Jesus Christ. It is normally seen as a time to be spent at home with one's family. Preparations often begin three or four weeks beforehand, as people decide what presents to buy for close family and friends.

A Christmas tree is usually decorated and installed in the entrance hall or living room, around which presents are placed before they are opened on Christmas Day. Christmas cards are normally sent to family and friends from the beginning of December. Non-Christians usually send cards too, which will often simply say 'Seasons Greetings'. Houses are decorated with special Christmas garlands, and sometimes a wreath of holly on the front door. Mistletoe is often hung above doorways, beneath which couples should traditionally kiss. Christmas is both a religious and a secular holiday, celebrated by believers and non-believers alike. Many families attend a church service, either at midnight on Christmas Eve, or on Christmas morning.

Children hang up a long sock, stocking, or pillowcase at the foot of their bed, or around the fireplace for Father Christmas to fill with presents. On Christmas Day families traditionally sit down to a dinner of roast turkey, followed by Christmas pudding – a rich steamed pudding made from suet, dried fruit and spices.

The British Father Christmas is a cheerful old man with a beard, dressed in a red suit trimmed with fur. He travels from an area close to the North Pole on a sledge pulled by reindeer, delivering presents to children. The Father Christmas we have today is often said to be based on folklore that Dutch, German and Swedish settlers brought to America, although there are a number of other rival theories explaining his origins.

Boxing Day, the 26th December, refers to a time when servants, gardeners, and other trades people used to receive money (a Christmas box) in appreciation for the work they had done throughout the year. Many people still give to postmen.

Boxing Day is a holiday in Britain, where people visit family and friends and continue with Christmas festivities. It is also a popular day for sporting activities – weather permitting.

New Year, January 1st, is celebrated in Britain, as it is in many countries throughout the world. Parties or celebrations begin on New Year's Eve, and when midnight arrives everybody cheers and drinks a toast for good luck in the coming year.

In Scotland, New Year can be a bigger festival than Christmas. Here there is a tradition in many homes of first footing, in which the first visitor of the New Year brings in particular items such as coal, bread and whisky intended to ensure prosperity for the coming year.

In Wales, on the stroke of midnight, the back door is opened to release the Old Year. It is then locked to keep the luck in, and at the last stroke, the front door opened to let in the New Year.

Easter, which takes place in March or April, commemorates the Crucifixion and Resurrection of Jesus Christ, although it is named after the Saxon goddess of spring, Eostre, whose feast took place at the Spring equinox. Easter, like Christmas, has become increasingly secular, and often taken as an opportunity for a holiday.

Easter eggs, made from chocolate (traditionally, decorated chicken's eggs) are given as presents, particularly to children, symbolising new life and the coming of spring. Some places hold festivals and fairs on Easter Monday.

REVISION QUESTIONS

Test your understanding of this section by completing the questions below. Check your answers on page 57

55	What is the Grand National?
	ANSWER:
56	What does the abbreviation FA stand for?
	ANSWER:
57	What is the name of the popular UK tennis tournament played in South London?
	ANSWER:
58	Which of the UK national days is celebrated with a holiday? Name the country where this is celebrated?
	ANSWER:
59	What and when are the national days of the four countries of the United Kingdom?
	ANSWER:
60	Name the patron saints of the four countries in the United Kingdom?
	ANSWER:
61	How many bank holidays are there each year in the United Kingdom?
	ANSWER:

62 When are Christmas presents opened?

ANSWER:

63 When is Christmas celebrated?

ANSWER:

64 What does Christmas day celebrate?

ANSWER:

65 What is mistletoe traditionally used for during Christmas?

ANSWER:

66 What is traditionally eaten on Christmas Day?

ANSWER:

67 Where does Father Christmas folklore originate?

ANSWER:

68 What does Boxing Day celebrate?

ANSWER:

69 When is New Year celebrated in the United Kingdom?

ANSWER:

70 If you were the first visitor of the New Year to a Scottish home, what might you be expected to bring?

ANSWER:

71 If you were visiting a Welsh home during the New Year, what tradition might be observed?

ANSWER:

72 What do Easter eggs symbolise?

ANSWER:

73 When is Easter celebrated?

ANSWER:

74 What does Easter commemorate?

ANSWER:

Other traditions

St Valentine's Day, February 14th, is the day when boyfriends, girlfriends, husbands, and wives traditionally exchange cards and presents; cards are unsigned as if from secret admirers.

Mothering Sunday, three weeks before Easter, is a day on which children, young and old, remember their mothers by giving them flowers or chocolates and trying to make their day as easy and enjoyable as possible.

April Fool's Day, April 1st, is the day when people may play jokes on one another – but only until 12 noon. Sometimes even radio, television, and newspapers try to fool people with fake stories and jokes. The tradition is believed to have originated in sixteenth century France.

Guy Fawkes Night, November 5th, commemorates the Gunpowder Plot in 1605 when a small group of Catholics are said to have plotted to kill the King by blowing up the Houses of Parliament. Soldiers arrested Guido (Guy) Fawkes who was allegedly guarding the explosives beneath Parliament. Today he is remembered with fireworks and the burning of a 'Guy' on a bonfire.

Remembrance Day, November 11th, keeps alive the memory of those who died in both World Wars and in later conflicts. Many people now hold a two minute silence at 11.00am in remembrance of this, for it was at the eleventh hour, of the eleventh day, of the eleventh month in 1918 that the First World War (often called the Great War) finally came to an end.

The terrible fighting in the fields of Northern France and Flanders devastated the countryside and, in the disturbed earth of the bomb craters, it was the poppy that was one of the first plants to regrow. So this blood-red flower has come to symbolise the sacrifice of those who fall in war.

Today, in the period before Remembrance Day, artificial poppies are sold in shops and on the streets, and many people wear them in their buttonholes in memory of the dead.

REVISION QUESTIONS

Test your understanding of this section by completing the questions below.
Check your answers on page 57

75 When is St Valentine's Day

ANSWER:

76 What traditionally happens on St Valentine's Day?

ANSWER:

77 When is Mothering Sunday?

ANSWER:

78 What traditionally happens on Mothering Sunday?

ANSWER:

79 When is April Fool's Day?

ANSWER:

80 What traditionally happens on April's Fools day?

ANSWER:

81 When is Guy Fawkes night?

ANSWER:

82 What does Guy Fawkes night commemorate?

ANSWER:

83 What does Remembrance Day commemorate?

ANSWER:

84 When is Remembrance Day?

ANSWER:

85 When did the First World War end?

ANSWER:

86 What tradition is observed in the period before Remembrance Day?

ANSWER:

HOW BRITAIN IS GOVERNED

The working system

Parliamentary democracy

The British system of government is parliamentary democracy. General elections are held at least every five years, and voters in each constituency elect their MP (Member of Parliament) to sit in the House of Commons. Most MPs belong to a political party, and the party with the largest number of MPs in the House of Commons forms the government, with the more senior MPs becoming ministers in charge of departments of state or heads of committees of MPs.

The Prime Minister

The Prime Minister (PM) is the leader of the party in power. He or she appoints (and dismisses) ministers of state, and has the ultimate choice and control over many important public appointments. The Prime Minister's leading ministers form the Cabinet. The Prime Minister used to be called (in the lawyers' Latin of the old days) 'primus inter pares', first among equals; but nowadays the office has become so powerful that some people liken it to the French or American Presidency, an office directly elected by the people for a fixed term.

However, a Prime Minister who is defeated in an important vote in the House of Commons, or who loses the confidence of the Cabinet, can be removed by their party at any time. This rarely happens, but when it does, the event is dramatic and the effects can be great. For example, Winston Churchill replaced Prime Minister Neville Chamberlain in 1940; and Margaret Thatcher was forced to resign in 1990, when she lost the confidence of her colleagues.

Modern Prime Ministers have their official residence at 10 Downing Street, and have a considerable staff of civil servants and personal advisers. The PM has special advisers for publicity and relations with the press and broadcasting media – all of which adds to the power of the Prime Minister over his or her colleagues. Government statements are usually reported as coming from 'Number Ten'. If something is directly attributed to the Prime Minister it is of special importance.

The Cabinet

The Cabinet is a small committee of about twenty senior politicians who normally meet weekly to decide the general policies for the Government. Amongst those included in the Cabinet are ministers responsible for the economy (the Chancellor of the Exchequer), law and order and immigration (the Home Secretary), foreign affairs (the Foreign Secretary), education, health, and defence. Cabinet decisions on major matters of policy and law are submitted to Parliament for approval.

The British constitution

To say that a state has a constitution can mean two different things in different countries. Usually it means a set of written rules governing how laws can be made, and setting out the rights and duties of citizens that can be enforced by a constitutional or supreme court. But sometimes there is no written constitution so that the term simply describes how a state is governed, what are the main institutions of government and the usual conventions observed by the government and the politicians.

The United Kingdom constitution is an unwritten constitution. But although no laws passed by Parliament can be directly challenged by any British court, there are restraints on government. Laws define the maximum length of parliaments, the electoral system, qualifications for citizenship, and the rights of non-citizens. There are the rules and procedures of Parliament itself, and interpretations of laws made by the courts in light of the traditions of the common law.

Sovereignty

A fundamental principle of the British constitution is 'the sovereignty of Parliament'. But nowadays decisions of the European Union have to be observed because of the treaties that Britain has entered into; and British courts must observe the judgements of the European Court and the new Human Rights Act. Textbooks are written on 'The British Constitution' and constitutional law, but no one authority will agree fully with another. Some constitutional disputes are highly political – such as what should be the composition and powers of the House of Lords and what is the best system of national and local elections.

Some reformers want a written constitution, as does the third largest party at Westminster, the Liberal-Democrats. But others, including the leaders of the Labour and Conservative parties, value historical continuity coupled with flexibility and have no wish for big issues to be settled by a constitutional court, as in the United States and many other democratic countries. But what holds the unwritten system together is that party leaders observe conventions of political conduct.

Conventions

Conventions and traditions are very important in British political life. For example, the second largest party in the House of Commons not merely opposes the Government but is called 'Her Majesty's Loyal Opposition'. It has a guaranteed amount of time in Parliament to debate matters of its own choice, and its rights are defended by the Speaker, who chairs proceedings in the House of Commons.

The Leader of the Opposition has offices in Parliament and receives financial support from the Treasury both for his or her office and for the Shadow Cabinet. These are senior members of the main opposition party who 'shadow' Government ministers in different departments. The Leader of the Opposition also has a constitutional status (that is why we use capital letters). He or she stands beside the Prime Minister on formal state occasions, as when the Queen opens Parliament or when wreaths are laid at the Cenotaph in Whitehall on Remembrance Day.

Question Time, when Members of Parliament may ask questions of government ministers, is another parliamentary convention. Questions to the Prime Minister by the Leader of the Opposition are usually lively and combative occasions, often widely reported.

A competitive party system

Under the British system of parliamentary democracy, candidates nominated by political parties, and sometimes individual independent candidates, compete for the votes of the electorate in general elections and by-elections. (By-elections are held to fill a vacancy when an MP resigns or dies in office). The struggle between the parties to influence public opinion, however, is continuous, and takes place not only at election time.

The role of the media

Proceedings in Parliament are now broadcast on digital television and recorded in official reports, known as *Hansard*. Although copies of this are available in large libraries and on the Internet, www.parliament.uk, most people receive their information about political issues and events from newspapers, TV and radio.

In Britain there is a free press – that is, one that is free from direct government control. The owners and editors of most newspapers hold strong political opinions and run campaigns to influence government policy. All newspapers have their own angle in reporting and commenting on political events. Sometimes it is difficult to distinguish fact from opinion. Spokesmen and women of all political parties put their own slant on things too – known today as 'spin'.

In Britain, the law states that political reporting on radio and television must be *balanced*. In practice, this means giving equal time to rival viewpoints. Broadcasters are free to interview politicians in a tough and lively fashion, as long as their opponents are also interviewed and treated in more or less the same way.

During a general election, the main parties are given free time on radio and television to make short party political broadcasts. In citizenship lessons in schools young people are encouraged to read newspapers critically and to follow news and current affairs programmes on radio and television.

REVISION QUESTIONS

Test your understanding of this section by completing the questions below. Check your answers on page 58

87	How often are general elections held in the UK?
	ANSWER:

88	What is the role of the Prime Minister?
	ANSWER:

89	What is the abbreviation MP short for?
	ANSWER:

90	What did the title of Prime Minister used to be called in Latin?
	ANSWER:

91	What happens to policy & law decisions once they have been agreed by cabinet?
	ANSWER:

92	Where is the Prime Minister's official residence?
	ANSWER:

93	Where are government statements usually reported as coming from?
	ANSWER:

94	What is the name of the ministerial position that is responsible for the economy?
	ANSWER:

95	What is the name of the ministerial position that is responsible for order and immigration?
	ANSWER:

96 What is the name of the ministerial position that is responsible for foreign affairs

ANSWER:

97 What is the Cabinet?

ANSWER:

98 How is it decided which party forms government?

ANSWER:

99 What type of constitution does the UK have?

ANSWER:

100 What is the second largest party in the House of Commons called by convention?

ANSWER:

101 What is the role of the Speaker in the House of Commons?

ANSWER:

102 What happens during Question Time?

ANSWER:

103 When are by-elections held?

ANSWER:

104 What is the name of the official reports of proceedings in Parliament?

ANSWER:

105 Can newspapers publish opinions and run campaigns to influence government?

ANSWER:

106 What laws exist regarding political reporting on radio and television?

ANSWER:

The formal institutions

Government and politics in Britain takes place in the context of mainly traditional institutions, law and conventions, which ensure the acceptance of electoral or Parliamentary defeat, and peaceful and reasonably tolerant behaviour between political rivals.

The institutional arrangements are a constitutional monarchy, the House of Commons, the House of Lords, the electoral system, the party system and pressure groups, the judiciary, the police, the civil service, local government, and the recent devolved administrations of Scotland, Wales and Northern Ireland, together with a large number of semi-independent agencies set up by the government, nicknamed quangos, and now officially called Non-Departmental Public Bodies.

A constitutional monarchy

Britain has a constitutional monarchy. Others exist in Denmark, Netherlands, Norway, Spain, and Sweden. Under a constitutional monarchy, the powers of the King or Queen are limited by either constitutional law or convention.

In Britain, the Queen or King must accept the decisions of the Cabinet and Parliament. The monarch can express her or his views on government matters privately to the Prime Minister, for example at their weekly 'audience', but in all matters of government must follow the Prime Minister's advice. The Queen or King can only, in a famous phrase, 'advise, warn, and encourage'. There would be a constitutional crisis if the monarch ever spoke out publicly either for or against government policy.

The present Queen has reigned since her father's death in 1952. The heir to the throne is her oldest son, the Prince of Wales. He has let his opinions be publicly known on a range of environmental and other matters, but when he becomes King he will be required to act and speak only in a ceremonial manner. Today there are some who argue that modern Britain should become a republic, with an elected President. However, despite public criticisms of some members of the royal family, the monarchy still remains important and popular among most people in Britain today as a symbol of national unity. People distinguish between the persons of the royal family and the institutions they represent.

The Queen is Head of State of the United Kingdom. She is also monarch or head of state, in both a ceremonial and symbolic sense, of most of the countries in the Commonwealth. The Queen has important ceremonial roles in this country, which include the opening and closing of Parliament. Each year at the beginning of a new parliamentary session she reads by tradition 'the Queen's speech' from a throne in the House of Lords, stating the Government's policies for the next session. Today however, these are entirely the views of the Prime Minister and the cabinet.

The monarch also gives the letters of appointment to holders of high office within the Government, the armed forces, and the Church of England, but always on the Prime Minister's advice.

The House of Commons

The House of Commons is the centre of political debate in Britain and the ultimate source of power. It shares the huge Palace of Westminster with the House of Lords. In medieval times, the House of Lords was the more powerful, and so you will still hear some commentators call the Commons, the *Lower House*, and the Lords, the *Upper House*. Today the Commons can always overrule the Lords who can only delay the passage of new laws.

The MPs who sit in the House of Commons are elected from 645 constituencies throughout the UK. They have a number of different responsibilities. They represent everyone in their constituency, they help create and shape new laws, they scrutinise and comment on what the Government is doing, and they provide a forum for debate on important national issues. If you visit the House of Commons you may find few MPs in the main debating chamber. That is because most work is done in committees – scrutinising legislation, investigating administration, or preparing a report on some important issue.

Visiting parliament

There are public galleries from which the public may listen to debates in both Houses of Parliament and many committees. You can write to your local MP to ask for tickets. There is no charge, but MPs only have a small allocation of tickets, so requests should be made well in advance. Otherwise, on the day, you can join a queue at the public entrance, but a waiting time of one or two hours is common for important debates. Getting into the House of Lords is usually easier. Ask the police officer at the same entrance where to go. Further details are on the UK Parliament website, www.parliament.uk

The Speaker

The Speaker of the House of Commons is an ordinary MP, respected on all sides, and elected by fellow MPs. He or she has the important role of keeping order during political debates in a fair and impartial way; of representing the House of Commons on ceremonial occasions; and of ensuring the smooth running of the business of the House.

The Whips

The Whips are small groups of MPs, appointed by their party leaders, to ensure discipline and attendance of MPs at voting time in the House of Commons. The Chief Whip commonly attends Cabinet or Shadow Cabinet meetings and will negotiate with the Speaker over the timetable and the order of business.

The House of Lords

The House of Lords is in the middle of big changes. Until relatively recently, the members were all peers of the realm; that is hereditary aristocrats, or people who had been rewarded for their public service – for example in war, the Empire or government. They had no special duty to attend the House of Lords, and many did not do so.

In 1957 a new law was passed, enabling the Prime Minister to appoint peers just for their own lifetime. These Life Peers, as they were known, were to be working peers, and were encouraged to attend debates in the House of Lords on a regular basis. Today those appointed as life peers have normally had a distinguished career in politics, business, law or some other profession. Recently hereditary peers had their general right to attend the House of Lords removed, but were allowed to elect a small number of themselves to continue to attend.

Life peers continue to be appointed by the Prime Minister although, by convention, always include people nominated by the leaders of the other parties. Senior Bishops of the Church of England are automatically members of the House of Lords, as are most senior judges. Life peers also include members of other Christian denominations and of other faiths – Jewish, Muslim, Hindu, Sikh, or Buddhist, as well non-believers and humanists. Today the main role of the House of Lords is to examine in detail and at greater leisure new laws proposed by the House of Commons, and to suggest amendments or changes. In this way the Lords may delay – but not prevent – the passage of new legislation.

The House of Lords also frequently debates issues which the Commons pass over or can find no time for. House of Lords' committees also, from time to time, report on a particular social problem or scrutinise some aspect of the workings of government.

To prevent a government from staying in power without holding an election, the House of Lords has the absolute right to reject any proposed law that would extend the life of a Parliament beyond the statutory five year period. However, if this were ever to happen, the House of Commons could first abolish the House of Lords, who could only delay such an act! This is very unlikely but illustrates how constitutional restraints in the United Kingdom depends more on conventions than on strict law.

The Electoral System

Members of the House of Commons (MPs) are elected by a 'first past the post' system. The candidate in a constituency who gains more votes than any other is elected, even if he or she does not have a majority of the total votes cast. In the House of Commons, the government is formed by the party gaining the majority of the seats, even if more votes were cast in total for the Opposition.

Under this system, the number of seats going to the winner is always proportionately greater than their total vote. For this reason, some people argue that the system should be changed to one or other form of proportional representation, as in Ireland and most parts of continental Europe. However, neither of the main UK parties favours this, saying that large majorities in the House of Commons guarantee strong and stable government, and that PR (proportional representation) would lead to coalitions and instability.

However, the Scottish Parliament and the Welsh Assembly were both set up with different systems of PR to ensure that they were not completely dominated by a single party, as can happen under a 'first past the post' system. Similarly, the use of PR for elections to the Northern Ireland Assembly is intended to stop the Unionist (many Protestant) majority of voters from taking all the posts of government, and ensure 'power sharing' with the Irish nationalist (overwhelmingly Catholic) parties. In elections for the European Parliament yet another form of PR was adopted to conform more closely to European Union practice.

REVISION QUESTIONS

Test your understanding of this section by completing the questions below. Check your answers on page 59

107 What are quangos?
ANSWER:

108 What famous phrase describes the level of expression that the monarch is restricted to when discussing government matters?
ANSWER:

109 Who is the current heir to the throne?
ANSWER:

110 In which year did the Queen Elizabeth II start her reign?
ANSWER:

111 Who is the Head of State of the United Kingdom?
ANSWER:

112 What is mentioned in the Queen's speech?
ANSWER:

113 What ceremonial duties does the monarch have?
ANSWER:

114 Who does the monarch give letters of appointment to at the opening of parliament?
ANSWER:

115 Where is the House of Commons?
ANSWER:

116 What other names have been used to describe the House of Commons and the House of Lords?
ANSWER:

117 What are the responsibilities of an MP
ANSWER:

118 How many constituencies are there throughout the United Kingdom?
ANSWER:

119 How can you visit Parliament?

ANSWER:

120 How is the Speaker of the House of Commons chosen?

ANSWER:

121 Who are the Whips?

ANSWER:

122 In the past, what was the only way that members could be appointed to the House of Lords?

ANSWER:

123 In what year did the Prime Minister gain powers to be able to appoint members of the Lords?

ANSWER:

124 What is a Life Peer?

ANSWER:

125 What is the main role of the House of Lords?

ANSWER:

126 What is the name of the system that governs how MPs are elected into the House of Commons

ANSWER:

127 What must a party candidate achieve in order to win their constituency?

ANSWER:

128 Can a party candidate win a constituency if they don't get the majority of votes?

ANSWER:

129 Where is proportional representation used in UK politics?

ANSWER:

The party system and pressure groups

The British political system is essentially a party system in the way that decisions are made and elections conducted. There is only a handful of independent MPs or MPs from smaller parties. The main political parties have membership branches in every constituency throughout Britain. Local party organisations select candidates, discuss policy, and canvas the voters in national, local and European elections. Annual national party conferences are carefully managed and well publicised events, where general party policy is debated, and where local parties can have a significant effect on the Parliamentary leadership.

Public opinion polls have also become very important to the leadership of each party. Party leaders know that they have to persuade and carry large numbers of the electorate, who are not party members, and who in recent years have become less fixed and predictable in their voting habits.

Political party membership in Britain has been declining rapidly in the last few years, perhaps as a consequence of greater consensus between the parties on the main questions of economic management, both seeking the middle ground so that differences of policy and principle are more difficult to perceive; or perhaps because people now, working longer hours and harder, and enjoying for the most part a greater standard of living, can or will give less time to public service. No one knows if this is a temporary or a long-term change. This, combined with falling turn-out in elections, especially among 18–25 year olds, has become a matter of general concern and is widely discussed in the press and in the broadcasting media.

Pressure groups

Pressure groups are organisations that try to influence government policy, either directly or indirectly. There are many such groups in Britain today, and they are an increasingly important part of political life. Generally speaking, ordinary citizens today are more likely to support pressure groups than join a political party. Sometimes people distinguish between 'pressure groups' and 'lobbies'. Lobbies or 'interest groups' are seen not as voluntary bodies of ordinary citizens but as the voice of commercial, financial, industrial, trade, or professional organisations.

The Judiciary

Since medieval times, judges have prided themselves on being independent of the Crown. Under the British system, judges can never challenge the legality of laws passed by Parliament, but they do interpret legislation and if a law contravenes our human rights, judges can declare it incompatible. The law must then be changed.

As a rule, judges in court normally apply the law in the same way as they have done in the past. This ensures that similar cases are dealt with in a consistent way. However there are times when the circumstances of a case have not arisen before, or when senior judges decide that existing judgements do not reflect modern society. In these situations, by their decisions, judges can create or change the law.

Judges in Britain are appointed by a Government minister, the Lord Chancellor, from nominations put forward by existing judges. The names proposed are those of senior lawyers who are believed to have the ability and judgement to do the job. In the last few years however, there have been demands – to which the government is responding – that this process should become more transparent, and clearer to members of the press and public. It is also felt that judges should be more representative of the public at large. Many argue that the judges are drawn from too narrow a section of society and that women and members of ethnic minorities are not sufficiently represented.

The Police

The police are organised on a local basis, usually with one force for each county. The largest force is the Metropolitan Police, with its headquarters at New Scotland Yard, which serves London. The police have 'operational independence' – the Government cannot instruct them to arrest or proceed against any individual. But their administration is controlled by police authorities of elected local councillors and magistrates, and by the role of the Home Secretary. An independent authority investigates serious complaints against the police.

The Civil Service

The Government is serviced by a large number of independent managers and administrators, who have the job of carrying out Government policy. They are also known as civil servants.

The key features of the civil service are political neutrality and professionalism. Before the mid-nineteenth century civil servants were appointed by ministers and had to be supporters of the party in power. Civil service reform began in the early 19th century, when the East India Company governed India. To prevent corruption and favouritism, candidates were required to pass competitive examinations. In the 1860s this system was extended to the Home Civil Service and continues with many modifications today.

Members of the British civil service today are permanent servants of the state, working for whatever party is in power. This neutrality is very important, but is sometimes a difficult balance to strike. Civil servants must warn ministers if they think a policy is impractical or even against the public interest; but must ultimately find a way of putting into practice the policies of the elected Government.

Political party officials tend to do everything they can to put Government policy in a favourable light. Civil servants may find themselves in a dilemma if they think that a minister is being too optimistic about the outcome of a particular policy, or asking them to do things specifically to discredit the Opposition. In the past, commentators suspected that civil servants too easily imposed their departmental policies on new ministers; but now the suspicion is often that civil servants can on occasion be pushed into open support for party policies they think to be either impractical or incompatible with other policies.

A major restraint on civil servants from becoming too politically involved is the knowledge that, if a general election brings another party to power, they will have to work with a new Government – and an entirely different set of aims and policies. When a General Election is pending or taking place, top civil servants study closely the Opposition's policies so that they are ready to serve a new government loyally.

Local Government

Towns, cities, and rural areas in Britain are administered by a system of local government or councils, usually referred to as local authorities. Many areas have both district and county councils, although large towns and cities tend to be administered by a single authority, called a borough, metropolitan district, or city council.

Local authorities are responsible for providing a range of community services in their area – such as education, planning, environmental health, passenger transport, the fire service, social services, refuse collection, libraries, and housing. Today local authorities in England and Wales have considerably less control over the organisation of these services than they did in the past.

What local government is required to do is called 'mandatory services', as decided by central government. Citizens can take them to court if they do not perform them: But there are also 'permissive services', though less than in the past; what they may do if they want to and can afford to do. In England and Wales local authorities may only offer permissive services if empowered to do so by government legislation. However in Scotland, under devolution, local authorities can do anything they are not explicitly forbidden to do. This is a simpler system to understand and operate, but financial constraints make the two systems more similar than might be supposed.

Most of the money for local authority services comes from the Government, provided through taxation. Only about 20 per cent is funded locally through the collection of council tax. There are strict systems of accountability, which determine how local authorities spend their money, and the Government is now beginning to explore how much some local services can be delivered by voluntary community groups. Some see this as diminishing the powers of local government but others see it as a way of involving more ordinary citizens in how their area is run.

Elections for local government councillors are held in May each year. Many – but not all – candidates stand as members of a political party. A few cities in Britain, including London, also have their own elected mayors, with increased powers to manage local affairs. Serving on the local council is still frequently the first step (but less so than in the past) to getting the local party to nominate someone as a candidate for election to the national Parliament or Assembly or to the European Parliament in Strasbourg.

Devolved administration

In 1997, the Government began a programme of devolving power from central government, with the intention of giving people in Wales and Scotland greater control over matters that directly affect them. Since 1999 there has been an Assembly in Wales, and a Parliament in Scotland, and the Government is now proposing the idea of regional governments in England where there is a clear local demand.

However, policy and laws governing defence, foreign affairs, taxation, and social security remain under the control of the UK Government in London, although these issues may be debated in the Welsh Assembly and the Scottish Parliament.

The National Assembly for Wales

The National Assembly for Wales is situation in Cardiff. It has 60 Assembly Members (AMs) and elections are held every four years. Members can speak in either English or Welsh and all its publications are in both languages. The Assembly does not have the power to make separate laws for Wales but it may propose laws for the decision of the UK Parliament in Westminster. However, it does have the power to decide on many other important matters, such as education policy, the environment, health services, transport and local government, where the present laws allow Welsh ministers a great deal of discretion in making detailed regulations.

The Parliament of Scotland

The Parliament of Scotland in Edinburgh arose as the result of a long campaign by people in Scotland for more independence and democratic control. For a long time there had been a devolved administration run by the Scottish Office, but no national elected body. A referendum for a Scottish Parliament, in 1979, did not gain enough support, but when another was held in 1997, the electorate gave a clear 'yes' both to establishing a Scottish Parliament and to it having limited powers to vary national income tax.

Today there are 129 Members of the Scottish Parliament (MSPs) in Edinburgh, who are elected by a form of proportional representation. Unlike the Welsh Assembly, the Scottish Parliament may pass legislation on anything not specifically reserved to Westminster (foreign affairs, defence, general economic policy, and social security).

The Scottish Parliament is funded by a grant from the UK Government and can spend it how it chooses. It has the legal power to make small changes in the lower base rate of income tax, which it has not exercised so far, and has adopted its own procedures for debate, the passage of legislation and access to the public – all deliberately different from the traditional ways of Westminster.

The Northern Ireland Assembly

The Northern Ireland Parliament, often called Stormont after the building where it met, was established in 1922, following the division of Ireland after civil war. Protestant political parties, however, dominated the Parliament, and abolished the electoral system of proportional representation that was designed to protect the Catholic minority – a community who faced considerable discrimination in housing and jobs in the public services.

The Government in London paid little attention to these problems until, 50 years later, protests, riots, and a civil disobedience campaign led them to abolish Stormont when reforms failed to materialise. Conflicts increased between Protestant and Catholic groups, the former determined to remain part of the United Kingdom; while the latter determined to achieve unity with the Irish Republic.

There followed many years of communal distrust, violence, and terrorism. But after a negotiated cease-fire by both the main para-military groups – the IRA (the Irish Republican Army), and the UDA (the Ulster Defence Associate) – the Good Friday Agreement was signed in 1998 between the main parties and endorsed by the Irish and British governments, working closely together.

Shortly afterwards, the Northern Ireland Assembly was established, with a power-sharing agreement in which the main parties divided the ministerial offices between them. The Assembly has 108 elected members, with powers to decide on matters such as education, agriculture, environment, health, and social services in Northern Ireland.

In view of the political situation in Northern Ireland, the UK government kept the power to suspend the Assembly if the political leaders could no longer agree to work together or if the Assembly was not working in the interests of the people of Northern Ireland. This has happened on a number of occasions.

Non-departmental public bodies

Much of government that affects us all is conducted not directly, but through a multitude of agencies with various degrees of independence. These are organisations that Parliament can create or abolish, or change their powers and roles, but are not a direct part of the civil service. They are sometimes called quangos – quasi-autonomous non-governmental organisations.

A few examples of non-departmental public bodies

Trading bodies set up by central government that raise revenue: Her Majesty's Stationery Office (official and semi-official publications), Forestry Commission, National Savings Bank, Crown Estates Commission.

Spending agencies funded by government: Regional Health Authorities, Higher Education Funding Councils, Sports Council, Arts Council, Legal Services Commission, Medical Research Council.

Quasi-judicial and prosecuting bodies: Monopolies and Mergers Commission, Criminal Injuries Compensation Authority, Police Complaints Authority, Crown Prosecution Service.

Statutory Advisory Bodies to Ministers: Gaming Board, Health and Safety Commission, Law Commission, Commission for Racial Equality, Equal Opportunities Commission, Advisory Board on Naturalisation and Integration.

Development agencies (many of which are public-private partnerships): Scottish Enterprise, Highlands and Islands Development Board (Scotland), Welsh Development Agency, Rural Development Commission, several regional Urban Development Corporations.

REVISION QUESTIONS

*Test your understanding of this section by completing the questions below.
Check your answers on page 60*

130 What is the distinction between a pressure group and a lobby group?
ANSWER:

131 Can a judge challenge the legality of a law?
ANSWER:

132 How are judges appointed?
ANSWER:

133 What is the name of the largest police force in the United Kingdom?
ANSWER:

134 Where are the headquarters of the Metropolitan Police force?
ANSWER:

135 How are the police structured and organised?
ANSWER:

136 Who controls the administration of the Police?
ANSWER:

137 What is a Civil Servant?
ANSWER:

138 What are the two key features of the civil service?
ANSWER:

139 When did the civil service begin?
ANSWER:

140 What is the responsibility of a local authority?
ANSWER:

141 Where do local authority services get their funding from?
ANSWER:

142 When are local government elections held?
ANSWER:

143	When did the government start a programme of devolved administration for Wales and Scotland?
	ANSWER:

144	Which areas of policy always remain under the control of the central UK government?
	ANSWER:

145	Where is the National Assembly for Wales situated?
	ANSWER:

146	How many Assembly Members are there in the National Assembly of Wales?
	ANSWER:

147	When was the second referendum for a Scottish Parliament?
	ANSWER:

148	When was the first referendum for a Scottish Parliament?
	ANSWER:

149	How many Members of Scottish Parliament (MSPs) are there?
	ANSWER:

150	What are the differences in power between the Welsh Assembly and the Scottish Parliament?
	ANSWER:

151	When was the Northern Ireland Parliament established?
	ANSWER:

152	What is the Northern Ireland Parliament often called?
	ANSWER:

153	When was the Good Friday Agreement signed?
	ANSWER:

154	How many members are there on the Northern Ireland Assembly?
	ANSWER:

Britain in Europe and the world

In addition to Britain's historical and cultural ties with countries throughout Europe, two major developments have occurred since the end of the Second World War in 1945 closely linking Britain to the remainder of Europe.

The Council of Europe

The Council of Europe was created in 1949, and Britain was one of the founder members. It is an organisation with 50 member states, working to protect human rights and seek solutions to problems facing European society today. The Council of Europe has no power to make laws, but does draw up conventions and charters, which member states agree to follow. Examples of these are the European Convention on Human Rights, measures to trace the assets associated with organised crime, and a directive for education for democratic citizenship in schools.

The European Union

The European Union originated in the period immediately after the Second World War when Belgium, France, Luxembourg, the Netherlands, and West Germany signed an agreement putting all their coal and steel production under the control of a single authority. An important reason for doing this was the belief that co-operation between these states would reduce the likelihood of another European war.

Britain refused to join this group at the beginning and only became part of the European Union (or European Economic Community, as it was then known) in 1973 after twice being vetoed by France. In 2004, ten new member countries joined the EU bringing membership to a total of 25.

The main aim behind the European Union today is for member states to become a single market. To achieve this, measures have gradually been introduced to remove tariff barriers and to help people, goods, and services move freely and easily between member states. This has involved a great deal of regulation being imposed on businesses and consumers, and has not always been popular.

Citizens of a EU member state have the right to travel to any EU country as long as they have a valid passport or identity card. This right may be restricted only for reasons of public health, public order, or public security. They also have the right to work in other EU countries, and must be offered employment under the same conditions as citizens of that state.

The Council of Ministers

The Council of Ministers is one of the most influential bodies in the EU. It is made up of government ministers meeting periodically from each member state with powers to propose new laws and take important decisions about how the EU is run.

The European Commission

Based in Brussels, the European Commission is rather like the civil service of the European Union, taking care of the day to day running of the organisation. One of the important jobs the European Commission is to draft proposals for new EU policies and law.

The European Parliament

The European Parliament meets in Strasbourg in north-eastern France. Each country elects members roughly proportional to its population. Elections for Members of the European Parliament (MEPs) are held every five years.

The Parliament scrutinises and debates the proposals, decisions, and expenditures of the Commission, but does not decide policy. MEPs have the ultimate power to refuse to agree EU expenditure, but have never done so – although they have held it up. Yet the threat has proved effective on several occasions.

European Union law

European Union law is an important source of law in Britain. EU legislation consists mainly of Regulations and Directives. Regulations are specific rules, such as those limiting the hours that drivers of goods vehicles can work, which automatically have the force of law in all EU member states. Regulations override national legislation and must be followed by the courts in each member state.

Directives are general requirements that must be introduced within a set time, but the way in which they are implemented is left to each member state. An example of this is the procedures that must be followed by companies when making staff redundant.

All proposals for new EU laws are examined by a committee of the UK Parliament, which then recommends any changes or amendments to ministers, who will decide whether to try and change or renegotiate them.

The Commonwealth

The Commonwealth arose out of the former British Empire that once included much of Africa and the West Indies, Canada, the Indian sub-continent, Australia and New Zealand. Since 1945, almost all these countries have become independent and together form a loose association called the Commonwealth, with the Crown at its symbolic head.

Only the United Nations is a larger international organisation than the British Commonwealth. The Commonwealth has a membership of 54 states, which together contain 1.7 billion people – 30 per cent of the world's population. Its aims include the development of democracy, good government, and the eradication of poverty, but it has no power over its members other than that of persuasion and only rarely acts together on international issues.

A common language, similarities in culture, and (with some exceptions) mutual recognition of professional qualifications, has greatly assisted the movement of people within the Commonwealth, and had a major effect on migration both to and from Britain.

The United Nations

Britain, like most countries in the world, is a member of the United Nations (UN) – an international organisation, working to prevent war and to maintain international peace and security. Britain is a permanent member of the UN Security Council The functions of this group include recommending action by the UN in the event of international crises and threats to peace.

Two very important documents produced by the United Nations are the Universal Declaration of Human Rights and the UN Convention on the Rights of the Child. Britain has signed and ratified both of these agreements. Although neither have the force of law, they are important measures by which the behaviour of a state can be judged, and they are increasingly used both in political debate and in legal cases, to reinforce points of law.

REVISION QUESTIONS

Test your understanding of this section by completing the questions below.
Check your answers on page 61

155 When was the Council of Europe established?

ANSWER:

156 What is the purpose of the Council of Europe?

ANSWER:

157 Describe the terms of the first agreement that European countries committed to, which lead to the forming of the European Union?

ANSWER:

158 When did Britain join the European Economic Community?

ANSWER:

159 What rights do citizens of European Union member states have to travel?

ANSWER:

160 What rights do citizens of European Union member states have to work?

ANSWER:

161 What is the Council of Ministers?

ANSWER:

162 Where is the European Commission based?

ANSWER:

163 What is the role of the European Parliament?

ANSWER:

164 What is the definition of an EU Directive?

ANSWER:

165 What is the definition of an EU Regulation?

ANSWER:

166 What is the population of all countries that are part of the Commonwealth?

ANSWER:

167 How many member states are there in the Commonwealth?

ANSWER:

168 What is Britain's role within the United Nations?

ANSWER:

169 What is the United Nations?

ANSWER:

The Ordinary Citizen

The right to vote

How does the ordinary citizen connect to government? As we have seen, full democracy came slowly to Britain. Only in 1928 did both men and women aged 21 and over gain the right to vote. The present voting age of 18 was set in 1969.

Both British born and naturalised citizens have full civic rights and duties (such as jury service), including the right to vote in all elections, as long as they are on the electoral register. Permanent residents who are not citizens have all civil and welfare rights except the right to hold a British passport and a general right to vote.

The electoral register

In order to vote in a parliamentary, local, or European election, you must have your name on the register of electors, known as the electoral register. If you are eligible to vote you may register at any time by contacting your local council election registration office. Voter registration forms are also available, in English, Welsh, and a number of other languages, via the Internet from the Electoral Commission, www.electoralcommission.org.uk

However the electoral register is also updated annually and an electoral registration form is sent to all households in September or October each year. The form should be completed according to the instructions, and should include everyone eligible to vote who is resident in the household on 15th October.

By law, a local authority has to make the electoral register available for anyone to look at. The register is held at the local electoral registration office (or council office in England and Wales) and some public buildings, such as libraries (however this is not always possible as new regulations require that any viewing of the electoral register is supervised, and libraries do not always have the necessary resources).

You have the right to have your name placed on the electoral register if you are aged 18 or over and a citizen of the United Kingdom, the Commonwealth, or a European Union member state. Citizens of the United Kingdom, the Commonwealth, and the Irish Republic resident in this country may vote in all public elections. Citizens of EU states, resident in the UK, have the right to vote in all but national parliamentary elections.

Participation

The number of people turning out to vote in parliamentary elections in Britain has been falling for several years, especially amongst the young. In the General Election of 2001, less than half of voters below the age of 25 actually voted. The Government and the political parties are looking for ways in which this trend might be reversed.

Standing for office

Citizens of the United Kingdom, the Irish Republic, or the Commonwealth aged 21 or over, may stand for public office. However, there are some exceptions, which include peers, members of the armed forces, civil servants, and those found guilty of certain criminal offices.

To become a local councillor, a candidate must have a local connection with the area, through work, by being on the electoral register, or through renting or owning land or property.

This rule, however, does not apply to MPs, MEPs, or to members of the Scottish Parliament, or the Welsh or Northern Ireland Assemblies. Candidates standing for these bodies must pay a deposit of £500, which is not returned if they receive less than five per cent of the vote. The deposit for candidates standing as a Member of the European Parliament is £5,000. This is to discourage frivolous or hopeless candidates, though many still try their luck.

Contacting elected members

All elected members have a duty to serve and represent the interests of their constituents. Contact details of all your representatives and their parties are available from the local library. Those of Assembly Members, MPs and MEPs are listed in the phone book and Yellow Pages. An MP may be reached either at their constituency office of their office in the House of Commons by letter or phone. The address: House of Commons, Westminster, London SW1A 0AA, tel 0207 219 3000.

Many Assembly Members, MPs and MEPs hold regular local 'surgeries', often on Saturday mornings. These are generally advertised in the local paper, and allow constituents to call in person to raise matters of concern. You can also find out the name of your local MP and get in touch with them by fax through the website, www.writetothem.com – this service is free.

REVISION QUESTIONS

Test your understanding of this section by completing the questions below.
Check your answers on page 62

170	What rights and duties do UK citizens have?
	ANSWER:

171	When did both men and women get the right to vote?
	ANSWER:

172	What is the current voting age and when was this set?
	ANSWER:

173	What are the basic requirements for standing for public office?
	ANSWER:

174	How and when do you register to vote?
	ANSWER:

175	How do you contact an elected representative?
	ANSWER:

REVISION ANSWERS

1   In the past immigrant groups came to invade and seize land. Now people come in search of jobs and a better life.

2   Irish labourers provided much of the workforce to construct the canals and railways of the UK.

3   Aid the reconstruction effort after the Second World War

4   Poland, Ukraine, Belarus

5   Ireland and the West Indies

6   1857

7   Women over the age of 30 got the right to vote in 1918. It wasn't until 1928 that women received the rights at the same age as men.

8   There are more women than men in university.

9   45 per cent

10   Three quarters of women that have children in the UK are in paid work.

11   Women receive on average 20 per cent lower pay than men.

12   15 million

13   25 per cent live in single parent families.
10 per cent live with a step family.

14   Compulsory tests are carried out at ages 7, 11, & 14.
GCSEs are carried out at 16. A Levels at 17 & 18

15   One in three move on to higher education

16   Two million

17   Tobacco must not be sold to anyone under the age of 16.
Alcohol must not be sold to anyone under the age of 18.

18   One in five

19   58.8 million

20   17 per cent

21   1.7 million

22   2.9 million

23   5.1 million

24   1801

25	2011
26	Because Britain was at war
27	Once every ten years
28	100 years
29	7.9 per cent of UK population
30	Indian descent
31	About half
32	29 per cent
33	45 per cent
34	70 per cent
35	3 per cent
36	75%
37	1534
38	The Anglican Church
39	Supreme Governor
40	The reigning King or Queen
41	The King or Queen takes advice from the Prime Minister based on a recommendation from a Church appointed committee
42	To maintain the protestant religion in the United Kingdom
43	Anyone who is not Protestant
44	The Kirk
45	10 per cent
46	Approximately 500 kilometres (320 miles)
47	Approximately 1,000 kilometres (600 miles)
48	Wales
49	Highlands and Islands of Scotland
50	1999
51	The Baptists and Methodists
52	London
53	Liverpool

54 Tyneside

55 A popular horse racing event

56 The Football Association

57 Wimbledon tennis championships

58 St Patrick's Day in Northern Ireland (and the Republic of Ireland)

59 St David's – Wales: 1 March
St Patrick's – Northern Ireland: 17 March
St George's – England: 23 April
St Andrew's – Scotland: 30 November

60 St David's – Wales
St Patrick's – Northern Ireland
St George's – England
St Andrew's – Scotland

61 Four bank holidays each year

62 On Christmas Day

63 25th December each year

64 The birth of Jesus Christ

65 Often hung above doorways under which couples are expected to kiss.

66 A roast turkey dinner and Christmas Pudding (containing fruit and spices)

67 Dutch, German, and Swedish settlers emigrating to America

68 Appreciation of work by servants and trades people – who are given a Christmas Box.

69 January 1st each year

70 Coal, bread, and whisky to ensure prosperity in the coming year.

71 The back door is opened to release the old year, then shut and locked, and then the front door opened to let in the New Year.

72 New life and the coming of spring

73 In March or April each year

74 The Crucifixion and Resurrection of Jesus Christ

75 February 14th each year

76 Couples send cards to each other. Cards are unsigned as if from secret admirers.

77   Three weeks before Easter.

78   People remember their mothers by giving gifts and flowers and try to make their day as enjoyable as possible.

79   April 1 each year

80   People play jokes on each other, but only until noon that day.

81   The evening of the 5th November

82   The Gunpowder Plot of 1605 – when a catholic group plotted to bomb the Houses of Parliament and kill the King.

83   The memory of those who died during war

84   November 11

85   Eleventh hour, of the eleventh day, of the eleventh month in 1918. (11 Nov 1918)

86   People wear artificial poppies in buttonholes in memory of those that lost their lives during war.

87   At least once every five years

88   Leader of the party in power. Also appoints ministers of state, and other important public positions.

89   Member of Parliament

90   *Primus inter pares* – meaning first among equals

91   They are submitted to Parliament for approval

92   10 Downing Street in London

93   "Number Ten"

94   Chancellor of the Exchequer

95   Home Secretary

96   Foreign Secretary

97   A committee of about 20 politicians that meet to decide general policies for government.

98   The party with the most MPs elected into the House of Commons forms the government.

99   An unwritten constitution

100   Her Majesty's Loyal Opposition

101 To chair the proceedings that take place in the House of Commons

102 Members of Parliament may ask questions with government ministers

103 Only held to replace an MP if they resign or die while in office

104 Hansard

105 Yes, Britain has a free press.

106 The law states that radio and television reports must be balanced – and must give equal time to rival view points.

107 Quasi-autonomous non-governmental organisations.
These are semi-independent agencies set up by the government.

108 The King or Queen can only "advise, warn, and encourage".

109 The Queen's oldest son, the Prince of Wales.

110 1952 – after her father's death.

111 The Queen.

112 A statement of the Government's policies for the next session. The statement is entirely provided by the Prime Minister.

113 Opening and closing of parliament and reading the "Queen's (or King's) Speech".

114 Holders of high office within the Government, the armed forces, and the Church of England.

115 In the Palace of Westminster

116 The Commons is sometimes called the Lower House, and the Lords, the Upper House.

117 Represent their constituency, help create and shape new laws, scrutinise and comment on government work, debate important national issues.

118 645

119 Tickets to the public galleries can be obtained from your local MP or by queuing on the day at the public entrance.

120 The Speaker is elected to the position by fellow MPs.

121 A small group of MPs that ensure discipline and attendance of MPs at voting time in the House of Commons.

122 By being either peers of the realm (hereditary aristocrats), or as a reward for special public service.

123 1957

124 A member of the House of Lords that has been appointed by the Prime Minister – but only for the member's lifetime.

125 To examine in detail and at greater leisure, the new laws proposed by the House of Commons, and to suggest amendments or changes.

126 The "first past the post" system

127 The candidate must win the most votes out of any of the other candidates. This does not need to be a majority.

128 Yes, the candidate that gets the most votes wins the constituency – even if this is not a majority.

129 In the Scottish Parliament, Welsh Assembly, and Northern Ireland Assembly. PR is also used in the European Parliament.

130 Pressure groups are a voluntary group of ordinary citizens. Lobby groups generally represent commercial, industrial, and professional organisations

131 No, although they may interpret legislation and if it contravenes human rights, then they may declare it incompatible and requiring change.

132 They are appointed by the Lord Chancellor, from nominations put forward by existing judges.

133 The Metropolitan Police.

134 New Scotland Yard in London

135 Each county has a force and is organised locally

136 Elected local councillors and magistrates and by the Home Secretary

137 Any independent manager or administrator that has a job requiring them to carry out Government policy.

138 Neutrality and Professionalism

139 In the early 19th century, when the East India Company governed India.

140 To provide community services in their local area – such as education, planning, health, transport, fire service, refuse collection, libraries, and housing.

141 From central government taxation. Only 20% is collected through council tax.

142 May each year.

143 The programme began in 1997.
There has been an Assembly in Wales and a Scottish parliament since 1999.

144 Policies governing defence, foreign affairs, taxation, and social security. This doesn't exclude these topics from being debated in other assemblies

145 In Cardiff

146 60 Assembly Members

147 1997

148 1979

149 129 Members of the Scottish Parliament

150 Unlike the Welsh assembly, the Scottish Parliament is able to pass legislation on anything not specifically reserved for Westminster.

151 1922

152 Stormont. After the building where the parliament meets.

153 1998

154 108 members

155 1949

156 To protect human rights and seek solutions to problems facing European society

157 To put all their coal and steel production under the control of a single authority. This was in the belief that it would reduce the likelihood of another war.

158 1973. This was after being vetoed twice by France.

159 Citizens of any EU member state have the right to travel to any EU country as long as they have a valid passport or identity card.

160 Citizens of any EU member state have the right to work in any EU country, and must be offered employment under the same conditions as citizens of that state.

161 An influential body in the EU made up of government ministers from each member state with powers to propose new laws and make decisions regarding the EU.

162 Brussels

163 To scrutinise and debate the proposals, decisions, and expenditure of the European Commission.

164 General requirements that must be introduced and observed within an EU member state within a specific time frame.

165 A specific rule that automatically has force in all EU member states, and that overrides national legislation.

166 1.7 billion people

167 54 member states

168 It is a member of the UN Security Council.

169 An international organisation that works to prevent war, maintain peace and security.

170 Full civic rights to vote in all elections and duties such as jury service.

171 1928

172 The current voting age is 18 years old. This was set in 1969

173 Must be a citizen of the United Kingdom, Irish Republic, or Commonwealth and be 21 years or over.

174 Complete an electoral registration form. These forms are sent to households in September and October each year.

175 By consulting details in your yellow pages, or local library. Alternatively visit the representative at a local 'surgery' session on Saturday mornings.

NOTES

241 (Urainian Ossociation)

King Street

(0208. 748 - 02441

tel 971 506 723667 ,,

154338 59930

Tel 0207 1320205